# Truman
# Capote

**The True Story of Feud: Capote vs. The Swans**

## EZEKSON PRESS

# Disclaimer

This biography is an independent publication that has been meticulously researched to provide a comprehensive account of the life and experiences of the individual in focus. It is not affiliated with any official organization, institution, or entity associated with the subject.

The information presented in this book is derived from a variety of sources, including historical records, interviews, and publicly available materials. While every effort has been made to ensure accuracy, the content is the result of an independent research endeavor and should be considered as such.

Readers are encouraged to verify and cross-reference information found within this biography, especially if it pertains to specific historical events, dates, or details. The author and publisher do not claim any official endorsement or authorization from the subject or their representatives, and this work is not intended to serve as an official biography.

This biography is a testament to the dedication and passion of independent authors and researchers who strive to shed light on the lives and legacies of remarkable individuals. It is offered to the public as a unique perspective on the subject and is intended for informational and educational purposes.

Thank you for your understanding, and we hope you find this independent biography insightful and engaging.

# Table Of Contents

# Introduction

Few rivalries have captured the public imagination as vividly as the famous quarrel between Truman Capote, the flamboyant literary maestro, and his once-devoted gang of gorgeous socialite friends known as the "Swans." This captivating story of friendship, treachery, and the pursuit of truth takes place against the backdrop of a bygone period, when richness and debauchery coexisted.

Truman Capote, known for his creative genius and effervescent personality, had close relationships with a group of affluent women known as the "Swans." These socialites, including Babe Paley, Slim Keith, and Marella Agnelli, were more than simply pals; they were muses, confidantes, and sources of inspiration for Capote's most well-known book, "In Cold Blood." However, the golden days of their brilliant alliance were broken when Capote's obsessive drive for literary achievement and appetite for gossip drove him to write a tell-all essay, "La Côte Basque 1965," which revealed the Swans' deepest secrets.

As the borders between fact and fantasy blurred, a furious feud broke out, tearing apart the fragile fabric of friendship that had once held them together. The consequences were both public and profound, as the Swans battled to reconcile their personal lives with the allegations made by their former confidant. In the aftermath of the incident, Capote found himself isolated from the very milieu that had previously welcomed him, forced to confront the implications of his uncontrolled pursuit of literary glory.

"Fued: Capote vs. Swans - Unraveling the Tapestry of Truth" digs into the complexity of this compelling story, examining the deep web of emotions, loyalties, and deceptions that marked Capote's connections with the Swans. As we travel through the hallways of wealth and the shadowy shadows of personal treachery, the story serves as a devastating reminder of the fleeting nature of celebrity, friendship, and the never-ending pursuit of truth.

# Who was Truman Capote?

Truman Capote, born in the dynamic metropolis of New Orleans in 1924, left an unmistakable effect on American literature as a multifaceted figure who excelled as a novelist, screenwriter, dramatist, and actor. His literary works include timeless classics like as "Breakfast at Tiffany's," now well-known for its film version starring Audrey Hepburn, and "In Cold Blood," a foundational work frequently attributed with sparking society's interest in true crime. Capote rose to prominence with the later novel, which he co-wrote with Harper Lee, a lifelong friend and fellow author.

Capote, known for his distinctive, high-pitched voice and unusual vocal mannerisms, carved out a niche for himself with an unorthodox style and a predilection for embellishments. His habit of professing familiarity with people he'd never met, such as Greta Garbo, added dimensions to his enigmatic presence. Capote's attraction extended beyond his literary prowess to include a predilection for alcohol and drug use. His varied social circle included authors, critics, business magnates, philanthropists, Hollywood and theater figures, monarchs, and high society members.

Amid the complexities of Capote's public life, a long-running feud with writer Gore Vidal became a distinguishing feature, causing Tennessee Williams to joke about their battle for an imaginary gold medal. While Capote never explicitly supported the gay rights movement, his candor about his own homosexuality made him a prominent figure in the cultural scene.

Truman Capote's life is a fascinating mix of creative genius, quirks, and societal dynamics, confirming his lasting legacy as a multidimensional and powerful American cultural hero.

# Who were Capote's Swans?

The Swans, an exclusive group of socialites synonymous with New York City's high society, boasted a glittering roster that included fashion luminaries such as Barbara "Babe" Paley (portrayed by Naomi Watts), Nancy "Slim" Keith (brought to life by Diane Lane), and C.Z. Guest (enacted by Chloë Sevigny), as well as royalty in the form of Lee Radziwill (portrayed by Calista Flockhart).

Babe Paley, the venerable grande dame of the Swans, played an important position in the exclusive circle as the wife of CBS pioneer William S. Paley, played by Treat Williams. Her prior job as a fashion editor for Vogue propelled her to the pinnacle of Manhattan's high society from the 1950s to the 1970s. She was inducted into the International Best Dressed List Hall of Fame in 1958 and maintained a glamorous image until her death from lung cancer in 1974.

Slim Keith, a seasoned veteran of the high life, was introduced to the social scene by Hollywood star William Powell. Her former husband, Howard Hawks, a formidable Warner Brothers mega-producer known for bringing Hollywood icons Lauren Bacall and Humphrey Bogart together, gave her the nickname "Slim". Keith, a member of Capote's Swans, distanced herself from the author in the 1980s after learning that the unflattering character Lady Coolbirth in "Answered Prayers" was a mirror of her own personality.

C.Z. Guest, another fashion icon, was a regular on best-dressed lists before being inducted into the Fashion Hall of Fame. Guest, known for her passion for horses, fashion, and gardening, partnered with Capote on a horticulture book, establishing her as a top hostess and inspiration for artists such as Andy Warhol and Salvador Dalí.

Lee Radziwill, the younger sister of former First Lady Jackie Kennedy, brought a touch of royalty to the Swans. Truman Capote, who was married to Polish aristocrat Prince Stanislaw Albrecht Radziwill from 1959 until 1972, was intrigued by Radziwill's opulent and glamorous existence, as well as her inherent beauty, which he held in high regard.

The Swans' roster expanded to include Ann Woodward (portrayed by Demi Moore), Gloria Guinness, Marella Agnelli, and Pamela Harriman. Each of these women had luxurious lifestyles, adding to the intriguing story of a social elite inextricably linked to Truman Capote's world.

# Answered Prayers were troubled from the beginning.

While Capote was initially excited to begin writing "Answered Prayers," the novel quickly fell to the wayside, eclipsed by another interesting endeavor. In 1959, Capote and his buddy Harper Lee set out to investigate the heinous murders of the Clutter family in rural Kansas. Originally intended as the foundation for a piece in The New Yorker, this investigative journey marked the beginning of a long story that culminated with the publishing of "In Cold Blood" in 1965. This comprehensive nonfiction crime novel, a huge success, not only claimed the title of best-selling book of the decade, but also propelled Capote to millionaire status, forever changing the face of narrative nonfiction.

By this point, Capote's popularity had smoothly merged him into the upper echelons of New York society. He enjoyed throwing lavish parties and gossiping with his small group of socialite confidantes, known as the Swans. This inner group included notable figures including Barbara "Babe" Paley, Lee Radziwill, C.Z. Guest, Slim Keith, Marella Agnelli, and Gloria Guinness. Their complex connections and shared secrets were poised to lay the basis for "Answered Prayers," assuming Capote could ever find the time to put his thoughts on paper.

In 1966, Capote and Random House signed a formal contract for the illusive book, which included a $25,000 advance and a January 1, 1968 deadline. However, as time passed, this deadline became a distant memory, forcing a series of revisions to the agreement, totaling four over the next decade. The financial stakes increased gradually, culminating in an extraordinary $1 million offer for a completed work in 1981.

Kelleigh Greenberg-Jephcott, the author of "Swan Song," throws light on Capote's fastidious nature, exposing a predilection for redoing entire paragraphs to improve just a few words, as well as episodes of crippling writer's block. However, even this meticulousness could not fully explain

Capote's strange tardiness with "Answered Prayers." The book appeared to be doomed from the start, with the contents of its first three chapters sealing its fate.

## Capote Received Cautionary Advice Regarding the Contents of the Book

Truman Capote envisioned "Answered Prayers" as a roman à clef, an intricately braided novel in which real people and places were disguised as fictional characters. In this literary project, his real-life pals played characters in stories filled with violent violence, sexual infidelity, drug use, and betrayal. The daring issue arose: why would Capote risk losing their support by releasing such a provocative book?

One motivating element was Capote's apparent decrease in popularity following the peak of "In Cold Blood." Commissioned articles for Rolling Stone remained unfinished, and his

1973 collection of nonfiction writings, "The Dogs Bark," garnered mixed reviews. In this context, a book like "Answered Prayers" emerged as a possible trigger, capable of recapturing the public's attention, for better or bad.

Capote made the first step by sending the suggested first chapter, "Mojave," to Esquire in 1975. Its publication, however without much controversy, featured subjects resembling his friends Babe Paley and her husband Bill, the CBS creator. Despite eventually deciding to remove this chapter from the novel, Capote, buoyed by the positive response, continued with the next piece, titled "La Côte Basque, 1965."

Gerald Clarke, Capote's biographer, expressed concern about how this future chapter would be accepted. While reading it as Capote swam casually in a pool on a raft, Clarke reflected, "I said, 'People aren't going to be happy with this, Truman.'" He said, "Nah, they're too dumb." "They won't know who they are." However, history would prove Capote astonishingly wrong, as the developing saga proved that the astute public was far from unaware of the identities entrenched in the contentious narratives.

# The Swans Swiftly Sever Ties with Capote

Following the publication of "La Côte Basque, 1965" in Esquire's November 1975 edition, Truman Capote quickly left New York City, drawn away by the demands of an upcoming film job in Los Angeles. However, the consequences of his literary implosion were irreversible. According to author Greenberg-Jephcott, the aftermath was equivalent to detonating a bomb, and Capote became a persona not grata, shunned by individuals who had formerly been his confidantes.

Babe Paley, who was suffering from lung cancer, chose to remain silent towards Capote, never speaking with him again. Notably, when she died of her illness in July 1978, Capote was barred from attending her funeral, leaving him conspicuously absent from a gathering to say goodbye to a former friend. Capote's attempts to contact Slim Keith by phone and cable were met with silence. Meanwhile, Vanity Fair says that Keith considered legal action against Capote for libel.

In a stunning twist, Ann Woodward, who had an infamous history involving the accidental killing of her husband in 1955, was discovered lifeless on October 10, 1975, only days before the contentious chapter was published. There was speculation that Woodward, who may have read an advance copy of "La Côte

Basque," committed suicide as a reaction to the representation of her life.

While Lee Radziwill, the sister of former First Lady Jacqueline Kennedy Onassis, maintained a more restrained approach to Capote and his work, she acknowledged his profound disbelief, adding, "He was absolutely shocked... he'd say, 'But I'm a journalist—everybody knows that I'm a journalist!'" I just don't think he knew what he was doing, because he paid for it." Capote, striving to defend the novel's artistic merit, expected that the public would reject its content. He asked, "What did they expect? I am a writer, and I use everything. Did all those folks believe I was there to entertain them? Despite Capote's subsequent release of two additional chapters, "Unspoiled

Monsters" and "Kate McCloud," permanent harm had already been done to the delicate fabric of his relationships and reputation.

## "Capote's life took a dark turn after 'La Côte Basque'."

Isolated from his once-loved circle of pals in café society, Capote sought solace in an increasingly dangerous dependency on narcotics and drink as coping techniques. According to Vanity Fair, he gained weight during this chaotic period while frequenting the famed Studio 54 nightclub, where he socialized with luminaries such as Andy Warhol, the multi-talented Liza Minnelli, and others.

According to PBS, Capote struggled with substance misuse during the 1970s, falling into a disturbing cycle of cocaine, tranquilizers, and marijuana. Multiple spells in rehabilitation facilities followed, with C.Z. Guest standing out as one of the few steadfast allies who accompanied him to a facility in Minneapolis in 1978. However, the uproar surrounding "Answered Prayers" aggravated Capote's problems, resulting in public bouts of alcoholism and seizures.

In a gloomy episode of The Stanley Siegel Show in July 1978, an obviously drunk Capote was directly questioned about his drug and alcohol problems. "What's going to happen unless you lick this problem of drugs and alcohol?" questioned the host, Stanley Siegel. Capote, possibly not completely grasping the gravity of the subject, said grimly, "The obvious answer is that I'll eventually kill myself."

By this point, a visibly troubled Capote had publicly admitted to stopping work on "Answered Prayers," alleging both a creative and a personal crisis. His long-term relationship with partner Jack Dunphy had deteriorated, and Vanity Fair reported that he was involved in a court dispute with another lover, John O'Shea. Capote accused O'Shea of fleeing with the manuscript for another chapter, "Severe Insult to the Brain." The lawsuit, brought in 1981, was finally dismissed.

## The whereabouts of the Answered Prayers manuscript remain shrouded in mystery.

Truman Capote, who was ill and exhausted, sought refuge in Los Angeles in August 1984, where he stayed with his longtime friend Joanne Carson, the second wife of the legendary late-night TV personality Johnny Carson. Carson discovered Capote in her guest bedroom on August 25, fighting to breathe and with a faint pulse. In his final minutes, Capote mumbled the phrases "Beautiful Babe" and "Answered Prayers," but died before paramedics arrived.

An unfinished version of "Answered Prayers," comprising the three chapters originally serialized in Esquire, appeared in the United Kingdom in 1986 and a year later in the United States. Despite this release, the fate of Capote's original, fully envisioned work remains unknown.

Capote offered Carson a key to an unknown safe-deposit box the day before his death, assuring her that the remaining chapters "will be found when they want to be found." Unfortunately, these mysterious chapters have never surfaced.

Another acquaintance, Joe Petrocik, claimed to have seen a whole manuscript from Capote and thought that the writer may have buried it at a Greyhound bus depot during his 1978 college tour. Alternatively, some hypotheses suggest that Capote deliberately destroyed the manuscript after finding it fell short of his lofty aspirations.

Biographer Clarke and others, on the other hand, believe Capote simply abandoned the project, probably due to the outpouring of criticism. Clarke compares the truncated "Answered Prayers" to other unfinished novels such as Charles Dickens' "The Mystery of Edwin Drood" or F. Scott Fitzgerald's "The Last Tycoon," arguing that it is tantalizingly incomplete yet substantial enough to be read, appreciated, and, to some extent, evaluated on its own merits.

In any case, the story surrounding "Answered Prayers" is a fascinating look into Capote's thoughts on friendship, social class, and the infamous conflict it sparked, leaving an unforgettable effect on the legacy of this legendary literary personality.

# What happened to Truman Capote?

Unsurprisingly, Capote's relationship with the Swans was irreversibly damaged by the seismic choice to publish the revelatory chapter. This brave move had far-reaching ramifications for his life, ushering in a period of tremendous transformation. Capote found consolation in narcotics as a result of the stormy aftermath, and as the late 1970s progressed, his battles with addiction drove him into rehabilitation.

"He then became a social outcast," Leamer said, reflecting on Capote's life after the contentious sections were published. "After that, he began drinking heavily and doing drugs, and he evaporated, never writing what he could have written. The book never existed. He purported to write it, but he didn't.

Capote's life spiraled downward until his death from liver illness in 1984. At the age of 59, the literary luminary's tragic death marked the culmination of a turbulent journey that began with the ill-fated decision to reveal the Swans' secrets, forever altering the course of his personal and creative legacy.

Made in United States
Troutdale, OR
07/24/2024

21516709R00022